# GERMAN MARITIME AIRCRAFT

What appear to be wheels on the back of this Arado 196's floats are water rudders used to manoeuvre the aircraft at sea, in this shot they are in the lowered position, comparison with other photographs will show the in-flight position. The aircraft is operated by 2/SAGr 128 whose code 6W can be seen aft of the cross (609/1925/21).

# BRYAN PHILPOTT
# GERMAN MARITIME AIRCRAFT

WORLD WAR 2 PHOTO ALBUM NUMBER 18

A selection of German wartime photographs from the Bundesarchiv, Koblenz

 **Patrick Stephens, Cambridge**

First published in 1981

**British Library Cataloguing in Publication Data**

German maritime aircraft.—(World War 2 photo
   albums; no. 18).
   1. World War, 1939–1945—Aerial operations,
   German—Pictorial works
   2. World War, 1939–1945—Naval operations,
   German—Pictorial works
   3. Airplanes, Military—History—Pictorial
works
   I. Title     II. Series
   940.54′49′43      D787

ISBN 0 85059 445 6 (casebound)
ISBN 0 85059 446 4 (softbound)

Photoset in 10 pt Plantin Roman. Printed in Great
Britain on 100 gsm Pedigree coated cartridge and
bound by The Garden City Press Limited,
Letchworth, Hertfordshire, SG6 1JS, for the
publishers, Patrick Stephens Limited, Bar Hill,
Cambridge, CB3 8EL, England.

# CONTENTS

**Acknowledgements**
The author and publisher would like to express their sincere thanks to Mrs Marianne Loenartz of the Bundesarchiv for her assistance, without which this book would have been impossible.

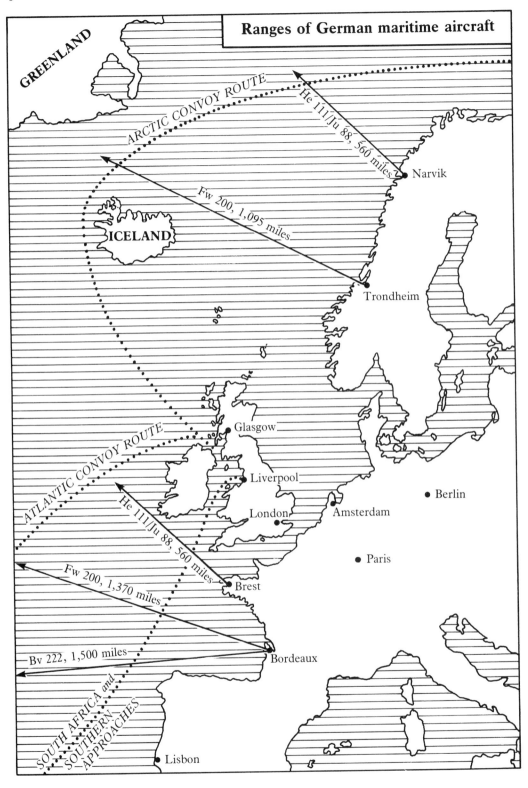

**Ranges of German maritime aircraft**

GREENLAND

ARCTIC CONVOY ROUTE

He 111/Ju 88, 560 miles

Narvik

Fw 200, 1,095 miles

ICELAND

Trondheim

Glasgow

Liverpool

ATLANTIC CONVOY ROUTE

He 111/Ju 88, 560 miles

London

Amsterdam

Berlin

Paris

Brest

Fw 200, 1,370 miles

Bv 222, 1,500 miles

Bordeaux

SOUTH AFRICA and SOUTHERN APPROACHES

Lisbon

In early 1939 a small maritime air force, whose main task was reconnaissance, existed under the control of the Kriegsmarine and it was known as the Seeluftstreitkräfte which, translated literally, means Fleet Air Arm. This force was unlike the Royal Navy's air element, as it had no carriers or aircraft designed specifically for the strike role or defence of the fleet at sea. The majority of the aircraft were seaplanes equipped for reconnaissance and having a minimum of defensive or offensive armament. Monitoring the sea lanes feeding German ports was not considered to be a task for the Luftwaffe, and little thought had been given as to how this force could be used in the maritime strike role, since it was considered by the planners to be primarily a tactical force operating in support of the army.

Most of the aircraft under the control of the Führer der Seeluftstreitkräfte were based in the Baltic and on the North Sea coast and comprised mainly three types all of which made their maiden flights in the mid-1930s. The He 59B, He 115 and Dornier Do 18, although appearing to be rapidly approaching obsolecence when war broke out proved, as did many other aircraft of similar vintage, to be more than suitable for the tasks set them and soldiered on long after their apparent usefulness was exceeded.

It was an He 59 which became the centre of controversy during the Battle of Britain when on July 9 1940 it was forced down near the Goodwin Sands by RAF Spitfires. The Heinkel was painted with Red Cross symbols and was claimed to have been on legitimate air-sea rescue duties. But it was escorted by a sizeable force of Bf 109s which claimed two Spitfires in the running fight leading to the forcing down of their charge, and was believed to have been monitoring shipping movements. The crew were rescued and made prisoners of war and the aircraft salvaged by the RAF. A few days later it was made quite clear to the Germans that any such aircraft, although marked with the international Red Cross, would be shot down if they were intercepted near convoys. Despite the shooting down of this and other white-painted, civil-registered aircraft, there can be no doubt that they were being used by the Seenotdienststaffel for air-sea rescue work which was particularly useful to the Luftwaffe Jagdgeschwarden operating over England and the Channel. There can also be little doubt that they were broadcasting information to Luftwaffe units and guiding dive bombers into the shipping lanes, therefore making themselves legitimate targets.

The He 59, like so many of the aircraft equipping German flying units at the outbreak of the war, had seen service in Spain with the Legion Condor where, in 1936, it had been used as a night bomber as well as in its designed role of shipping reconnaissance. There were several versions of the 77-foot span biplane which was powered by two BMW 12-cylinder, liquid-cooled engines, but a wheel version never reached production status. It was a classic between-the-wars biplane design accommodating a crew of four and able to take on the torpedo attack role if necessary. Although by the time World War 2 started considerable rethinking had to be carried out as far as the dropping of torpedoes from slow flying biplanes was concerned, the He 59 was used in a training role both in its designed capacity and for pilot, observer and radio operator training. It also performed other more militant tasks such as the clandestine dropping of agents, mine-laying in the Thames Estuary and along the English eastern seaboard, as well as acting in the tactical support role. In the latter category one of the most notable events occurred on May 10 1940 when 12 aircraft carrying a force of 120 troops took off from Lake Zwischenahn near Oldenburg and landed either side of the Willems Bridge near the centre of Rotterdam. This bridge, together with those over the Maas at Leeuwen and Jan Kuiten, were secured for the loss of four of the Heinkels, which was a small price to pay for the tremendous advantage secured for the advancing German army.

But all this was far ahead in mid-1939 when the Luftwaffe General Staff finally decided that they should have a force of bombers capable of carrying out specialised anti-shipping strikes. In the spring of 1939 General Hans Geisler became responsible for the formation of an anti-shipping strike force, which it was also envisaged could undertake the attacking of naval installations. Both being tasks which service rivalry and prejudices prevented units of the Seeluftstreitkräfte from carrying out. Geisler and his staff came under the control of Luftflotte 2 and on the outbreak of war his command was upgraded to Fliegerdivision 10 and a former naval officer, Major Martin Harlinghausen, became the operations officer. This officer had considerable experience of anti-shipping operations, much of it having been gained in the Spanish Civil War, and his influence was reflected in all future Luftwaffe shipping operations. One of the earliest techniques introduced by Harlinghausen was based on an old naval principle that ships presented the best target when approached directly from abeam; and with his staff operations officer, Hauptmann Robert Kowalewski as his pilot, he was very quick to lead the Geschwader Staff Flight in such raids. Approaching at low level aircraft presented a very difficult target for ships' lookouts, but at the same time the ships with their high superstructures were silhouetted against the horizon and gave the bomb-aimers enormous targets. In early 1940 aircraft engaged in operations of this type were mainly He 111s and Ju 88s operated by two Gruppen of KG 26 and one Gruppe of KG 30, and their success can be gauged from their claims of over 1,300,000 tons of Allied shipping sunk during the first year of war. Post-war records indicate that this figure was more than three times the amount of tonnage actually lost to air attacks, none the less it still represents a considerable figure to a force that was non-existent six months before the war started and had to perfect its methods from operational experience.

As well as the standard Luftwaffe level bombers, the notorious Ju 87 was used in the anti-shipping strike role and featured prominently during the Dunkirk withdrawal and the Battle of Britain. But, although their techniques were equally applicable to land or sea targets, range was a very limiting factor and such aircraft could obviously only attack shipping which was operating within reachable distance of their land base. In many respects the Ju 87 was an ideal aircraft, since to aim the whole machine at the target and allow for evasive action was a lot easier than bombing from a level bomber. In the English Channel and the approaches to Malta, Ju 87s

achieved a lot of success especially against merchantmen, but when air cover was present or effective anti-aircraft fire was available, the Ju 87 suffered.

Range limitations also created problems for the He 111 and Ju 88s and it was not until the FW 200 arrived on the scene that this major problem was resolved. Developed from the civil airliner used pre-war by Lufthansa, the FW 200 Kondor immediately extended the range of operations from 600 miles to over 1,000 thus bringing a new threat to Allied convoys operating far out in the Atlantic and southern approaches. The Kondor was able to carry a maximum bomb load of 4,626 lb which, in the early days, crews used with devastating accuracy claiming the sinking of 85 ships totalling 363,000 tons in the six months from August 1940 to February 1941. But the aircraft was structurally weak and very vulnerable to attacks from underneath since all its fuel feed lines were located in this position; weaknesses which did not entirely endear the aircraft to its crews, especially when the Beaufighter and Mosquito long-range fighters operated by Coastal Command of the Royal Air Force began operating in the Atlantic and the Bay of Biscay later in the war.

The FW 200's introduction into Luftwaffe service was the responsibility of Oberstleutnant Edgar Petersen who was ordered by Luftwaffe Chief of Staff, General Hans Jeschonneck, to establish a long-range anti-shipping squadron using ten modified FW 200s, four of which were unarmed. The unarmed aircraft were used as transports during the Norwegian campaign, which was a task more akin to their designed role, but in April 1940 armed versions mounted their first maritime patrol when they accompanied He 115 flying boats of Kü Fl Gr 506 on reconnaissance patrols over the North Sea. Petersen's aircraft operated as a Fernaufklärungsstaffel until the end of April 1940 when they formed 1/KG 40. Two months later 1 Staffel was redesignated I Gruppe, re-equipped with the FW 200C-1, and moved to Bordeaux-Mérignac where it saw action in the Battle of Britain. The Kondor was the only long-range land-based maritime aircraft used by the Luftwaffe and as such operated in many roles and theatres, including Iceland, Russia and the Atlantic where it earned its main reputation. As the war progressed and convoys became protected, initially by aircraft launched by catapult from the decks of merchantmen, then small escort carriers, losses mounted but they never reached proportions serious enough drastically to curtail operations. As convoy defence increased the Kondors, which were equipping three Gruppen of KG 40, were from time to time forced into modifying their tactics which gradually changed from singleton operations to those mounted by up to six aircraft being vectored to their targets by a reconnaissance Kondor shadowing the convoy out of range of its anti-aircraft defences. Such changes underline the efficiency achieved by the Allied countermeasures for, by mid-1943, attacks were made at heights of about 9,000 feet so as to avoid anti-aircraft fire; a far cry from the early days when Harlinghausen's low-level attacks reaped success for the Luftwaffe. The activity against Allied shipping by the Luftwaffe Kampfgeschwarden did not go unnoticed by the Seeluftstreitkräfte, who soldiered on with their floatplanes and flying boats in an attempt to make some worthwhile contribution.

An early, and unusual, success for a floatplane came on May 5 1940 when Leutnant Günther Mehrens flying an Arado Ar 196A-3 intercepted the British submarine HMS *Seal* in the Kattegat and captured it. The submarine, under the command of Lieutenant Commander R. Lonsdale, had been damaged by mines and was unable to dive. Mehrens attacked to such effect with his bombs and cannon that the submarine's skipper surrendered his boat, whereupon the German pilot landed alongside, picked up the unfortunate Captain and flew him to interrogation and captivity. The *Seal* was taken in tow by the Kriegsmarine to Friedrikshafen.

The aircraft involved in this incident was a popular low-wing floatplane which saw considerable service with the Luftwaffe and Kriegsmarine flying units. Design work commenced in 1937 and various prototypes with different float arrangements were tried before the twin-float layout was accepted for production versions. The crew were accommodated under a long greenhouse canopy and the observer /gunner faced the rear with a defensive 7·9 mm MG 17, which on later models in service was replaced by an MG 15. Fixed armament was initially the ubiquitous 7·9 mm MG 17 but on later versions a pair of 20 mm MG FF cannon were provided in the wings and defensive armament was increased to a pair of 7·9 mm machine-guns in the rear cockpit.

The aircraft entered service in 1939 and was issued to the German warships, *Gneisenau*, *Lützow*, *Scharnhorst*, *Prince Eugen*, *Bismark*, *Tirpitz*, and others. The *Bismark*'s machine was used during the famous action in the Atlantic, to intercept the shadowing RAF flying boats, not the first or last occasion when the aircraft was used in such a role. Bordfliegerstaffeln 1 /196 and 5 /196 were the first units to receive the Arado and the latter used them to effect in the Bay of Biscay under the control of Fliegerführer Atlantik where they gave U-boats cover from patrolling Coastal Command Whitleys. The floatplanes carried out this task with enough success to cause some worry to the Allies and the threat was not finally removed until the Beaufighter came on the scene as a more than adequate countermeasure.

Norway and the Aegean also proved useful hunting grounds for the aircraft which, in addition to its reconnaissance duties, could also carry a small bomb load. Operating as part of Luftflotte 1, Fliegerführer Ostee had 2 /SAGr 125 equipped with the Ar 196 and these were used against Russian targets as well as convoys operating in northern waters. This particular unit was much travelled, exchanging the arctic conditions of the Russian campaign for the sunshine of the Mediterranean where it arrived via the Baltic and Rumania. Despite its frail appearance the Arado was a sturdy aircraft capable of taking a lot of punishment; it also had a good amount of manoeuvreability which surprised many a fighter pilot who fell into the trap of underestimating his adversary. One unit was still equipped with the aircraft at the end of the war and fortunately examples survived and can now be seen in museums in the USA and Bulgaria.

The Seeluftstreitkräfte gradually found increasing opposition to its activities and, despite the enthusiasm of the officers manning the aircraft and devising operations, there was a constant fear that either the Kriegsmarine or Luftwaffe would absorb or terminate their tasks. This was eventually to come about in July 1942 when it was dissolved but by this time a significant contribution had been made and one which Hermann Göring recognised. This was the sea mining of coastal waters and estuaries which had been devised as early as April 1939 by General Joachim Coeler. This officer experienced a tremendous uphill struggle, mainly against the Kriegsmarine, but his persistence was rewarded when his mining operations were given the go-ahead by the Oberkommando der Kriegsmarine (Ob d M), albeit on a limited scale. Prior to this approval Coeler's units had needed permission from individual Kriegsmarine commanders in whose areas they intended to operate. The new clearance still tended to limit their mining operations to those specifically approved by the Ob d M, but gradually control was relaxed and the He 59s, Do 17s and He 111s began to operate with more independence. Coeler was able to put forward such a strong argument in favour of sea mining, proving that losses were minimal in relation to the successes achieved, that eventually Göring decided to create a Luftwaffe command with the specific responsibility for mining. This came into existence in February 1940 and was known as Fliegerdivision 9; it immediately assumed responsibility for all development of aircraft and tactics relating to sea mining and was thus instrumental in sealing the fate of the Seeluftstreitkräfte. As units became seconded to the Luftwaffe the original character of the service became absorbed into the 'new' flying service, so the disintegration of the Seeluftstreitkräfte and its ultimate demise can be traced directly to one of its keenest supporters and most able officers.

Aircraft operated by Seeluftstreitkräfte units were taken over by the Luftwaffe and many of the original naval airmen also transferred their allegiance, although throughout the war it was not unusual to have a mixed naval and Luftwaffe aircrew operating together. The Luftwaffe's growing anti-shipping strike force was used in an attempt to blockade Britain and in this role it worked very closely with Grossadmiral Dönitz's U-boats. It was in such operations far out in the Atlantic that the FW 200 Kondor really came into its own since its range and loiter time enabled it to shadow convoys and report their movements to U-boat Captains. On some occasions the roles were reversed, this usually happening when a U-boat commander followed a convoy and reported its track and position to the Luftwaffe. Although these activities took a heavy toll of merchantmen they failed to achieve the disruption of the convoy systems hoped for and by mid-1941 it was realised that what the Luftwaffe had failed to achieve over England in 1940 would also not be achieved by joint Luftwaffe Kriegsmarine operations at sea.

During the spring of 1941 a complete re-organisation of Luftwaffe commands had been carried out with the sole intent of concentrating all anti-shipping units along the European coast to carry out the task previously outlined, when this failed units were dispersed to the Mediterranean, Norway and inevitably the Russian front, and were used either in conventional bombing roles or in the anti-shipping role against coastal ships and harbour installations.

While Luftwaffe planners were involved in devising tactics most suitable for anti-shipping operations, there was still a political argument as to who should control the units involved. An example of the heights this reached being indicated by Hitler's personal intervention in January 1941 when he gave total control of I /KG 40 to Dönitz. This decision was reversed in March when the re-organisation took place but it was not a true reversal since KG 40 now came under the command of Harlinghausen who was the first Fliegerführer Atlantik, and as such was primarily responsible to Dönitz for supplying cover and reconnaissance for U-boats.

The co-operation between U-boats and the Luftwaffe certainly enjoyed mixed fortunes but the increasing Allied strengths and the continual 'borrowing' of Luftwaffe anti-shipping units to carry out night bombing raids to appease the German public, saw a gradual diminishing of the anti-shipping role. When Harlinghausen was wounded in October 1941 and only replaced by a deputy, the importance of his command declined.

Harlinghausen recovered from his wounds and was appointed head of development for the supply, training and operational use of the aerial torpedo. This was a weapon which was sadly lacking in the maritime aircraft's inventory before the war, and in the opening years its development had been somewhat hampered by the inevitable service rivalry. Original research and experiments had been started in 1938 by the Kriegsmarine who had acquired the Horten naval torpedo from Norway as well as patented designs from Italy, but progress was slow and when the Luftwaffe took an interest the Kriegsmarine refused to make their results available to them.

In January 1942 Harlinghausen took up his command and by the spring I /KG 26 was undergoing training with He 111-6s which had been adapted to carry torpedoes on racks beneath the fuselage. The use of this aircraft conveniently solved the problem of a suitable carrier, for although it was purely an adaptation of an existing design, it was much more efficient than some of the proposed solutions which included the old He 115 flying boat.

The new weapon proved most effective and when Allied convoys started plying the Arctic route KG 26's He 111 torpedo-carrying aircraft took a heavy toll. The system evolved was simplicity itself and depended on a shadowing aircraft relaying position reports to the strike aircraft, these reports enabled the leader of the strike aircraft to formate into his best attack position before reaching the convoy, as well as keeping him well advised of any course changes or other alterations which might affect the interception. The standard pattern of torpedo attack was for the Heinkels to approach at their most economical cruising speed in two or three Vic formations, on arriving in the convoy area and having decided the best approach they would form into line abreast and approach at approximately 150 feet, each aircraft releasing its weapons against a chosen target. The torpedoes would be dropped with a short interval between each and the aircraft would make its escape at low level by increasing speed after the release point and jinking through the convoy. Early morning or dusk attacks were favoured as these conditions not only silhouetted the ships but also gave some protection to the aircrafts' crews.

The torpedo, as already stated, proved an effective weapon but it must be viewed in perspective with maritime operations of the period; taken in isolation it can be considered to have been unsuccessful, and bearing in mind the problems of the precision approach and dropping methods needed this is probably true. But on a much narrower appraisal it certainly caused problems to some convoys, especially PQ 18 which lost eight ships to torpedo attack from He 111s in the autumn of 1942. This was probably the most notable success achieved by this method of attack and by 1943 improved defences coupled with tactical limitations saw the decline of the use of torpedoes.

Operations in the Arctic mirrored tactics used by the anti-shipping force in every theatre, the increased Allied activity in the Middle East culminating with the North African landings brought intense aerial operations over the Mediterranean as attempts were made to cut off the sea supply route.

Once again long-range reconnaissance aircraft featured prominently and alongside the FW 200 the Blohm and Voss Bv 138 made a significant contribution.

After a disappointing entry to service when structural weaknesses were mainly responsible for its bad reputation, the aircraft recovered to perform effectively in not only the long range reconnaissance role but also as a minesweeper and strike aircraft. The Bv 138 was a somewhat ponderous flying boat with a crew of six and a maximum duration of 18 hours. Like its counterpart, the Short Sunderland, it could give a good account of itself in battle and on one occasion one aircraft fought a 90-minute running battle with Sea Hurricanes when it was intercepted shadowing a PQ convoy in the Arctic, and lived for the crew to tell the tale. Bv 138s ranged far and wide and it was not unknown for them to be refuelled by U-boats at sea, thus increasing their patrol times. One notable operation which took place in the late summer of 1943, was the flying from the Soviet island of Novaya Zemlya by a pair of Bv 138s. These aircraft carried out several patrols from this Soviet held island on which U-boats had set up a forward base, and were able to monitor movements in the Kara Sea for a period of 21 days before they were recalled to a more secure base.

Versatility such as this was achieved by many of the flying boats and floatplanes operated by the Luftwaffe and their story would fill many pages; it is a story that would be well worth telling and perhaps one day a book will be devoted to it. In this brief summary it must simply be stated that flying boats and seaplanes performed many varied tasks very efficiently and formed a vital part of German maritime operations. The Bv 138 was followed into service by its big brother the six-engined Bv 222 which made its debut in military colours in December 1941. The Bv 222 was the largest flying boat to serve in World War 2 and although never available in any great quantity it carried out useful tasks initially in the trooping configuration – a natural progression from its intended civil use with Lufthansa – and latterly in the long-rang reconnaissance role. There were, of course, many other flying boats worthy of mention, among them being the Dornier Do 18 and 24, the former featuring in an early action when an aircraft from 2 /Kü Fl Gr 106 spotted the *Ark Royal*, *Hood*, *Nelson*, *Rodney* and *Renown*, and was able to get off a position report before being shot down by a Skua from the *Ark*, thus becoming the first Luftwaffe aircraft to be destroyed by British aircraft in World War 2. The Do 18 also saw service during the Battle of Britain and although gradually being phased out during 1941-2, it did useful work in the air-sea-rescue role. Its larger three-engined brother, the Do 24, had a chequered career having been used by the Dutch against the Japanese in the Far East before it entered Luftwaffe service. The aircraft's main task was air-sea-rescue and it had a fairly uneventful war.

Like most other fields of operations the maritime strike force operated by the Luftwaffe produced its personalities; one of them was without doubt Oberst Harlinghausen, but perhaps the most well known is Werner Baumbach who became General of Bombers by the end of the war.

Baumbach served with I /KG 30 from the very outset of the campaign in 1939 and progressed with the unit from the North Atlantic to the Mediterranean during which time he devised tactics and carried them out to such effect that he was decorated with the Knight's Cross with Crossed Swords. By mid-1943 the tactics devised by Harlinghausen and Baumbach, although still sound, were proving very difficult to carry out and a new anti-shipping weapon was desperately needed. This came about in the form of a pair of air-launched guided weapons, one being the Fritz-X stand-off bomb, and the other the Henschel Hs 293 glider bomb. The first of these to be used against shipping was the Hs 293 which had a wing-span of 10 feet and carried a 1,100 lb warhead; it was released by the carrier aircraft at a height of 5,000 feet and using its own liquid fuel rocket accelerated to a speed of 370 mph in a 12-second motor run, after which it descended in an accelerating glide to its target. Controlled by a small joy-stick on board the parent aircraft, the Hs 293 had an effective range of about five miles, although this did vary according to the height at which it was released, and a flare attached to its tail gave visual indication of its position. Penetration of armour was not possible due to the low (sic) impact speed of the missile, so its main use was against merchant ships.

Dornier Do 217E-5 aircraft of II /KG 100 used the Hs 293 for the first time in the autumn of 1943 and in November of the same year II /KG 40 used their newly acquired He 177A-5s as carrier aircraft

to launch 16 Hs 293s against convoy SL139 /MKS 30. This action resulted in the loss of one ship, which was in any case a damaged straggler, and three He 177s, thus making it a costly exercise as far as the Luftwaffe was concerned. Five days later II /KG 40 suffered more when four out of eight He 177s, including the aircraft flown by Major Mons the Gruppenkommandeur, failed to return from another glider bomb attack against a convoy off Bougie. This loss caused the unit to abandon daylight operations in favour of night attacks in which a pair of aircraft would drop flares while another pair released their Hs 293s from a range of six to nine miles. This successfully reduced losses but also reduced the strike rate thus making the whole operation nothing more than a nuisance raid in which a ship might be sunk or damaged.

The Fritz-X was an entirely different concept being a free-falling bomb with small wings half-way along its length and a total weight of just over 3,000 lb. It was usually released from a height of 16,000 feet and aimed by a conventional bombsight through which the operator made adjustment by radio-controlled stabilisers during its final trajectory; visual guidance again being provided by a tail-mounted flare.

Although both these weapons achieved some initial success and the delivery aircraft were not as vulnerable as those engaged on, for example, torpedo attacks, the time immediately after release proved troublesome as the parent machine had to fly a reasonably straight and level course to enable the guidance operator to carry out his function. This, coupled with the fact that if fighters intercepted the carrier before it released its missiles evasion was practically impossible, considerably reduced the impact of these two weapons. None the less, credit must be given to the Germans for introducing such advanced (for the time) weapons and tactics, which really only failed to achieve notable success because they came too late; too late because the Allies were able to offer a quick counter. Also, as with many other similar episodes, forward planning to provide a modern aircraft to carry such a weapon had not been carried out.

The effect the Luftwaffe maritime units had on the last two years of the war is negligible when taken in its broadest context; after the European invasion strike, units were used against land targets and on mining operations, but although some ships were sunk and problems were caused to military movements, the force was fairly ineffective. The last few months of the war saw the same problems occurring in maritime units as they did in all others, plenty of aircraft, inexperienced crews, and very little fuel, a trio of circumstances which could in no way be combined to produce viable results.

To sum up the whole war as far as maritime aircraft operations are concerned, it is enough to say that lack of forward vision in planning Luftwaffe maritime operations, inter-service rivalry, insufficient modern design seaplanes, the continual use of land based aircraft against land targets after they had been trained in maritime operations, the late introduction of an efficient aerial torpedo, and a totally misguided belief that the few units involved could put the British navy out of action, all played a significant part. However, the crews, like their counterparts in other Luftwaffe units and theatres, always gave of their best when in their hearts many must have seriously doubted the wisdom of their leaders.

The photographs in this book have been selected with care from the Bundesarchiv, Koblenz (the approximate German equivalent of the US National Archives or the British Public Records Office). Particular attention has been devoted to choosing photographs which will be fresh to the majority of readers, although it is inevitable that one or two may be familiar. Other than this, the author's prime concern has been to choose good-quality photographs which illustrate the type of detail that enthusiasts and modellers require. In certain instances quality has, to a degree, been sacrificed in order to include a particularly interesting photograph.* For the most part, however, the quality speaks for itself.

The Bundesarchiv files hold some one million black and white negatives of Wehrmacht and Luftwaffe subjects, including 150,000 on the Kriegsmarine, some 20,000 glass negatives from the inter-war period and several hundred colour photographs. Sheer numbers is one of the problems which makes the compilation of a book such as this difficult. Other difficulties include the fact that, in the vast majority of cases, the negatives have not been printed so the researcher is forced to look through box after box of 35 mm contact strips – some 250 boxes containing an average of over 5,000 pictures each, plus folders containing a further 115,000 contact prints of the Waffen-SS; moreover, cataloguing and indexing the negatives is neither an easy nor a short task, with the result that, at the present time, Luftwaffe and Wehrmacht subjects as well as entirely separate theatres of operations are intermingled in the same files.

There is a simple explanation for this confusion. The Bundesarchiv photographs were taken by war correspondents attached to German military units, and the negatives were originally stored in the Reich Propaganda Ministry in Berlin. Towards the close of World War 2, all the photographs – then numbering some $3\frac{1}{2}$ million – were ordered to be destroyed. One man in the Ministry, a Herr Evers, realised that they should be preserved for posterity and, acting entirely unofficially and on his own initiative, commandeered the first available suitable transport – two refrigerated fish trucks – loaded the negatives into them, and set out for safety. Unfortunately, one of the trucks disappeared en route and, to this day, nobody knows what happened to it. The remainder were captured by the Americans and shipped to Washington, where they remained for 20 years before the majority were returned to the government of West Germany. A large number, however, still reside in Washington. Thus the Bundesarchiv files are incomplete, with infuriating gaps for any researcher. Specifically, they end in the autumn of 1944, after Arnhem, and thus record none of the drama of the closing months of the war.

The photographs are currently housed in a modern office block in Koblenz, overlooking the River Mosel. The priceless negatives are stored in the basement, and there are strict security checks on anyone seeking admission to the Bildarchiv (Photo Archives). Regrettably, and the author has been asked to stress this point, the archives are *only open to bona fide authors and publishers, and prints can only be supplied for reproduction in a book or magazine.* They CANNOT be supplied to private collectors or enthusiasts for personal use, so *please* – don't write to the Bundesarchiv or the publishers of this book asking for copy prints, because they cannot be provided. The well-equipped photo laboratory at the Bundesarchiv is only capable of handling some 80 to 100 prints per day because each is printed individually under strictly controlled conditions – another reason for the fine quality of the photographs but also a contributory factor in the above legislation.

* Due to unknown reasons, a particularly high proportion of Bundesarchiv photographs of maritime aircraft are scratched or incorrectly exposed or focused. Nevertheless, many of these have been included in this volume due to their intrinsic interest.

**Right** There is much of interest in this close-up of a Norwegian-based Ar 196. The ETC 50 wing rack is empty and the wing-mounted 7·9 mm machine-gun has its barrel blanked off. The trolley and paint demarcation on the float struts are also of interest (514/363/11a).

# THE PHOTOGRAPHS

**Above** Flown for the first time in August 1937 the He 115 was already obsolete when war started. None the less it was a popular aircraft with crews and carried out sterling work operating mainly from Norwegian bases. The large size of the aircraft is very evident in this view of an He 115B–1 of 1/Kü Fl Gr 206 (MW/5402/15).

**Below** A recognition characteristic of the He 115 was its large square fin and rudder which is very evident in this B–1 which belongs to Kü Fl Gr 506 (MW/5537/32).

**Above** The badge on this He 115B–1 consists of a brown cup and three white dice and is the emblem of
1 Staffel Kü Fl Gr 206. The code M2 was used by Kü Fl Gr 106 which was the first coastal patrol group
to operate the He 115 in Norway (MW/5402/10).

**Below** This He 115C, K6 + EH belongs to 1/Kü Fl Gr 406 and is fitted with a 15 mm MG 151 cannon
under the nose, the bulbous fairing is for the collection of spent shell cases (514/352/36a).

**Above** Kü Fl Gr 406 was the first unit to attack the ill-fated convoy PQ 17 using its He 115s which were later supported by Ju 88s, He 111s and U-boats. This B–1 of the unit patrols over typical Norwegian scenery (514/367/15a).

**Below** A Kü Fl Gr 406 crew pose before their He 115C–1 in which the offset mounting of the 20 mm MG 151 cannon can be clearly seen. The centre figure is an Oberleutnant but the scarves and fur collars of the other two keep their ranks a secret (514/351/36).

**This page** A busy scene featuring He 115C–1 K6 + RH of 1/Kü Fl Gr 406 undergoing repair in a Norwegian fjord in late 1942. The aircraft has the 20 mm MG 151 fitted in the cupola under the nose and reinforced planing surfaces to the floats. A white disruptive pattern has been painted over the dark green top surfaces and the undersides of the wing tips are yellow. All under surfaces are light blue (514/352/7 and 4a).

**Left** The comfort of the interior of a hangar contrasts with some of the field conditions in which aircraft had to be attended to. This He 115 is undergoing a major overhaul which conveniently reveals the internal structure of the fin/rudder assembly (MW/5538/27a).

**Below** These two He 60Cs of 1/SAGr 126 are lashed down, with cockpits covered, control locks in place, and oil drums providing land anchorage. They were photographed on one of the Greek islands among which they patrolled during the day (433/890/26a).

**Opposite page** A sesquiplane of mixed wood and metal construction, the He 114 was developed alongside the better known He 115, and operated as a coastal reconnaissance machine. It saw service over the Channel, North Sea, Mediterranean and Adriatic but its activities were confined to areas of little enemy fighter activity. These two examples, which are C–1 versions, were operated in the Black Sea area by the Rumanian air force and served with 101 and 102 Coastal Reconnaissance Squadrons (611/2131/24a and 635/3979/21a).

**Background photograph** Designed in 1930 as a torpedo-bomber, the He 59 made its operational debut in the Spanish Civil War. It went on to serve the Luftwaffe in many roles including reconnaissance, bombing, air-sea rescue and training. This is a B–2 version with dark green upper surfaces, light blue under surfaces, yellow rudder and engine cowlings (431/721/2a).

**Inset** The He 59 was already an anachronism when the war started. None the less it achieved many notable successes including the transportation of 60 troops to capture the main Rotterdam bridge. It also achieved notoriety when it was used as an air-sea rescue machine painted with red crosses but carrying out clandestine reconnaissance as well as its claimed role. This aircraft is an He 59B–2 carrying the insignia of the international Red Cross (MW/5402/39).

**Left** The exposed nose gun position of the He 59 and its 7·9 mm machine-gun adds interest to the foreground as this He 59B–2 is towed from its mooring (344/730/30).

**Below** The steam boat, yacht and air of tranquillity lend an atmosphere of peaceful summer days; only the camouflage and markings of the He 59B–2 bring the reader back to reality and the days of World War 2. The enormous size of the wooden and metal twin-engined biplane can be appreciated by the figures standing alongside the port float (357/1857/28a).

**Right** Air-sea rescue was an essential task carried out by the He 59, and fortunately a camera was on hand to record the recovery of this lucky airman. The 7·9 mm machine-gun and its mounting ring as well as the forward windows are all very clear, as is the gunner's life vest and protective clothing (343/669/36a).

**Below right** 'Oh dear.' The circumstances surrounding the demise of this particular He 59 are not known, but it is clear that there is a lot of work in hand for someone (MW/1074/14a).

**Above** Sun, spray and a seaplane; ingredients which cause many a nostalgic look to a past era which hopefully will never be forgotten. The aircraft is in fact a floatplane He 59B–2 whose twin 7·9 mm MG 15s in nose and dorsal turrets provided some protection against fighters, but achieved more as morale boosters to the crews (343/669/25a).

**Below** An He 59B–2 M2 + RW of 3/Kü Fl Gr 106 is lifted from the water by a travelling gantry crane. The huge underwing crosses are worthy of note (335/25/38a).

**Above left** A lot of useful detail in this close-up of one of the floats on an He 59. The absence of a life jacket shows supreme confidence on the part of the crewman, or perhaps a flagrant disregard for official orders which stated that life support vests should be worn at all times in or near operational float/seaplanes (344/730/28).

**Above right** The dorsal-mounted 20 mm Hispano-Suiza 404 cannon mounted in the turret of this Do 24T comes in for attention from two sure-footed armourers (434/910/20a).

**Below** One of the two 12-cylinder Vee liquid-cooled BMW engines of an He 59B. The recessed exhaust system, maze of bracing wires, and the seemingly very small mounting on the lower mainplane, are all details which are normally overlooked in more general views of the aircraft (344/730/13).

**Above** A Laté 298D of the Vichy navy taxis past a Dornier 24. The French-built and designed floatplane was a sturdy machine which performed well in the early days of World War 2 before the French surrender. It was used as a dive bomber to attack bridges and road junctions during the German advance, and its structure enabled it to take a lot of punishment and survive (430/681/18).

**Below left and this page** The Luftwaffe captured Laté 298s of the 6ᵉ Flottille during the occupation of Vichy France but spares proved to be a problem even after the aircraft was put back into production in March 1942. This French floatplane also operated in conjunction with RAF Wellingtons in hunting and killing submarines (430/681/19, 431/720/29a, 431/720/23a).

**Left** Fokker T VIII floatplanes fell into Luftwaffe hands after the Lowlands campaign in 1940. Although lacking some of the qualities sought by the Luftwaffe and Kriegsmarine, they were put into service in communications and reconnaissance roles. The unit insignia of 1/SAGr 126, a Dutchman with a spyglass, is painted on the nose of this T VIII (433/890/19a).

**Below** He 60s and Fokker T VIIIs of 1/SAGr 126 all carrying the unit's insignia in various positions, at their Aegean base. The nearest Fokker has its starboard American-built Wright engine removed, the attainment of a spare from the manufacturers probably being a major problem for maintenance personnel! (433/890/15a).

**Right** The long greenhouse canopy, loop aerial and unusual position of the pitot head on the pilot's windscreen, are all evident in this view of a 1/SAGr 126 Fokker T VIII. The pilot's gun sight can also be seen just forward of the port side windscreen (433/890/14a).

**Below right** One of the better-known Luftwaffe flying boats was the Blohm and Voss Bv 138. This C version belongs to SAGr 130 operating in Norwegian waters, and has disruptive white camouflage daubed over its dark green upper surfaces including the national markings (507/104/25a).

**Left** A Feldwebel checks one of the connections of the fuelling hose from the front hatch of a Bv 138C (507/102/4a).

**Top** Rendezvous with a U-boat off the Norwegian coast by a radar-equipped Bv 138C of SAGr 130 (506/97/7a).

**Above** A crew tender awaits alongside a Bv 138C of 3/SAGr 125. Note also the mooring buoy attached to the nose of the aircraft (635/3973/22a).

**Right** An Unteroffizier takes flight rations aboard a Bv 138 (507/105/16a).

**Far left** The radio operator's station on board a Bv 138. The equipment is mounted on the port side of the fuselage so this view is taken looking forward towards the flight deck (498/18/31a).

**Left** Celebration time for a Bv 138 Captain on the completion of his 250th sortie (498/18/5a).

**Below left** This Bv 138C–1 rides gently at anchor as the crew, just visible by the cockpit hatch, fit all its protective covers in place. The cover over the 20 mm MG 151 in the bow turret emphasises the size of the barrel (506/92/36).

**Bottom left** A crewman secures the rope for the tender via the front hatch located forward of the turret which housed a 20 mm MG 151 cannon (498/18/3a).

**Right** Belts of 20 mm ammunition being taken aboard a Bv 138C–1 by two 'blackmen'. The aircraft was a stable gun platform and its defensive armament was very effective both in this role and when used offensively (498/20/28).

**Below** A choice of exit is taken by this Bv 138 crew as they scramble aboard a floating jetty from the cockpit roof hatch and bow entry of this Bv 138C–1 (498/18/14a).

**Background photograph** The central Jumo engine had its radiator intake immediately below the airscrew, while the wing-mounted units had theirs further back under the wings, this is clearly visible in this view of a moored Bv 138C which also has the cowling of its starboard engine in the open position (499/73/3a).

**Inset left** All Bv 138Bs and Cs could be fitted with a pair of 1,100 lb thrust rockets to assist take-off, the installation of these pods can be clearly seen under the port wing of this particular aircraft (498/25/31a).

**Inset right** The FuG 200 Hohentweil radar aerials of this Bv 138C–1 rendezvousing with a U-boat in a Norwegian fjord, are just visible inboard of the port engine (507/104/28a).

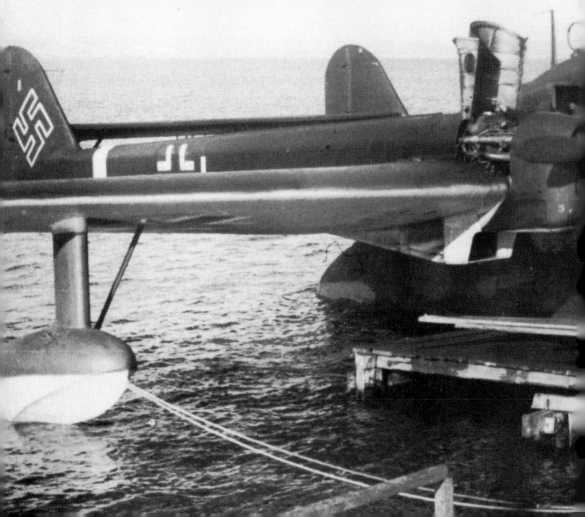

**Above left** The Bv 138 is being attached to the U-boat perhaps for a short tow or maybe just security as stores are transferred. Examination of the original print shows the pilot's seat is occupied and the crewman standing in the stern has a pair of flags similar to those being waved in the foreground (506/99/77).

**Left** The stern of this U-boat dips under the surface as its screw turns to take the strain of this Bv 138 of SAGr 130 (507/102/26a).

**Above** Tales of the sea or the air? Maybe a little of both as Luftwaffe flying boat crews swop stories (637/4198/13).

**Right** Out of their element most seaplanes look clumsy and inelegant. The Bv 138 was no exception although there is something very pleasing about the hull shape of this delicately balanced example (609/1925/32).

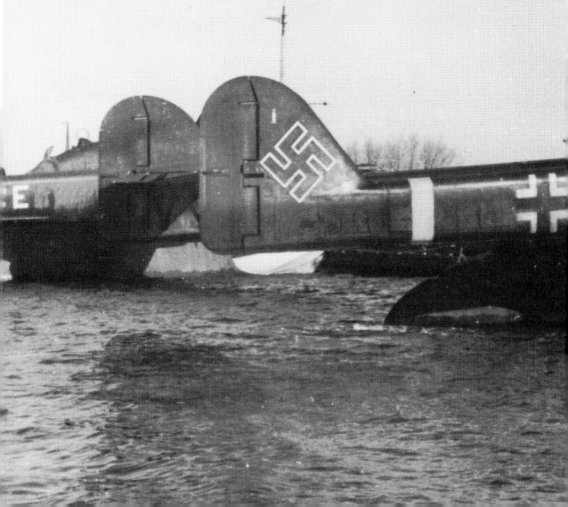

**Background photograph** Access hatches open, bow turret in the stowed position, add atmosphere to a Bv 138B as it awaits attention from its ground or aircrew. The Bv 138 had a range of well over 2,000 miles and great consideration was given at the design stage to ease of maintenance with the result that even relatively major repairs could be carried out at sea by the aircrew (499/73/24a).

**Inset left** On the step. With engines at full power this Bv 138B is just about to exchange the sea for the sky and adopts a classic pose so loved by flying boat enthusiasts (499/52/18).

**Inset right** The starboard wing float of a Bv 138 frames the wing-mounted depth charges as this boat sets out on patrol (499/65/25a).

**Above** This Bv 138 creates an interesting bow wave as it returns from patrol and taxis to its mooring (499/52/29).

**Left** Hull shape and bow turret, which is turned to the stowed position, are very clear on this Bv 138 which is beached for routine maintenance (498/20/2b).

**Above right** A popular Luftwaffe flying boat, the Dornier Do 24 adds a suitable background as the crew of G 'Gustav' a Bv 138B come ashore (499/65/11a).

**Right** The white disruptive camouflage applied to the hull of this Bv 138C–1 reveals its temporary nature in this pleasing view of a rendezvous between two U-boats and an aircraft of SAGr 130. Part of the radar array can just be seen forward of the empty wing racks, and the low profiles presented by the U-boats are also of interest (507/105/17a).

**Left** One of the Junkers Jumo six-cylinder diesel engines of the Bv 138 comes in for close scrutiny. The aircraft was able to carry four 330 lb depth charges on wing racks, and two of them can be seen adjacent to the engine's radiator intake (499/73/5a).

**Below** A Bv 138C–1 of SAGr 125 on patrol over the Arctic convoy routes (637/4797/23a).

**Right** Another classic shot, of a Bv 138C–1 on the step, which really needs no further comment (499/52/17).

**Below right** This is a very interesting picture as the Bv 138 shown is one from a very early production batch and is probably a Bv 138A–0. The centre engine carries only a three-bladed airscrew and the positions of the loop aerial and communications aerial mast are reversed from that of the B and C models (636/4054/10a).

**Above** This aircraft is almost certainly a Bv 138A–0 possibly on acceptance test at the Erprobungsstelle Travemünde. Note the three-bladed airscrew on the centre engine, also the reversed positions of the loop and communications aerial mast (636/4056/22a).

**Left** This is the same aircraft as shown in the previous picture and this close-up clearly reveals that a dummy turret is fitted in the bow position (636/4056/21a).

**Below and right** Port and starboard profiles of 7R + PL a Bv 138C–1 of 3(F) SAGr 125 on a shipping protection patrol over the Black Sea in 1943 (611/2134/27 and 31a).

**Below right** A Bv 138C–1 of SAGr 125 sends a white frothing spray across the calm waters of the bay as it reaches the point of take-off (637/4198/29).

**Above** The Bv 138 was known as the 'flying clog', its distinctive shape shown to advantage in this ground-to-air shot, clearly shows the similarity between the shape of the hull and the wooden shoe from which the nickname was derived (637/4197/18a).

**Left** This crew of 3(F)SAGr 125, whose badge shows a penguin astride a clog, have a very welcome reception committee awaiting them as they disembark from their Bv 138C–1 (635/3978/37a).

**Above right** The two rear gun positions, housing a 13 mm MG131 in the top and a 20 mm MG 151 in the turret, are clearly seen on this Bv 138C–1 of SAGr 125. At the time this photograph was taken the unit was operating from Rumania (637/4198/15).

**Right** Two Rumanian officers speak with a Leutnant as a Bv 138C–1 of 3/SAGr 125 runs up its port engine, at a Black Sea base in 1943 (635/3977/15).

**Left** A Rumanian officer swops cigarettes with a Feldwebel. The aircraft in the background is a CRDA Cant Z 501 Seagull (635/3979/32a).

**Above** The bomb-carrying penguin aboard a clog, which formed the basis of 3/SAGr 125's badge, adorns the battered hull of a Bv 138C–1 operating from the Black Sea in 1943. The officer flanked by the two much-decorated Rumanian officers is a Luftwaffe Leutnant (635/3977/18).

**Below and next page** In June 1940 Italy had 202 CRDA Cant Z 501 Gabbiano seaplanes in service, after the Armistice in 1943 the co-belligerent air force continued to use them and in fact, it was not until 1950 that the last example was taken out of service in Italy. The Gabbiano (Seagull) was of mixed wooden and metal construction, carried a crew of five, had three 7·7 mm Breda machine-guns, one of which was mounted in an exposed position on top of the engine nacelle, and could carry a load of 1,400 lb. Bombs were carried on racks attached to the bracing between the wings and hull and can be clearly seen on one of these photographs depicting an aircraft in Luftwaffe hands being operated from a base on the Black Sea (635/3978/3, 9A, and 10).

**Above** A Bv 138C–1 is towed from the shore to deep water ready for take-off. The outboard engines are idling and a crewman monitors the tow from the aircraft's lower stern turret. The wings carry splinter camouflage but it is difficult to tell, especially on the tailplane, where the official camouflage pattern ends and weathering begins (637/4198/16).

**Right** Good detail of the DF loop and communications aerial mast of a Bv 138 (499/56/25).

**Above** The angular cockpit framing of the Ju 52 somehow seems to reflect the overall appearance of the 'Tante Ju'. The pilot is wearing a very early-war style kapok-filled life jacket (643/4755/4a).

**Below** The pilot of a Bv 138 and his office. There is a clock mounted on top of the control column and the six basic blind flying instruments can be seen on the panel immediately in front of the pilot (498/20a).

**Above left** Another interesting view of the Bv 138 main office which, in this case, shows the throttles and pitch controls to the pilot's right (499/53/12).

**Above right** The ill-fitting tunic and seemingly very coarse material of the Feldwebel on the left contrasts with the leather flying clothing of the aviator with whom he is sharing what seems to be an amusing story (635/3979/23a).

**Below** A makeshift pathway provides reasonably sure footing for these Do 24 crewmen as they make their way to their aircraft (636/4054/43a).

**This page** A quiet moment for lunch and a letter from home for crewmen serving with Bord Fl Stf 1/196 whose sea-horse insignia is painted on a storage tank. The hut is built on the stone jetty alongside which the tender is being moored, and in the foreground can be seen the float of an He 60C with which the unit was equipped at this time. Two Staffeln (1 and 5) of Bordfliegergruppe 196 were formed at Wilhelmshaven in 1937 for shipboard use and were later re-equipped with the Arado Ar 196 (344/730/38, 34 and 32).

**Above right** The man under the engine nacelle has his hands clasped firmly to his ears, which is not surprising as the tandem-mounted Jumo 205C diesels seem to be running at something more than a tick-over. The aircraft is a Do 18D–1 and carries the three seagull badge of 1/Kü Fl Gr 506 (MW/5611/13a).

**Right** What appear to be odd markings on this Kü Fl Gr 506 Do 18D–1 are in fact shadows cast by the gantry. The dorsal gun position carried a 7·9 mm MG 15 (MW/5611/11a).

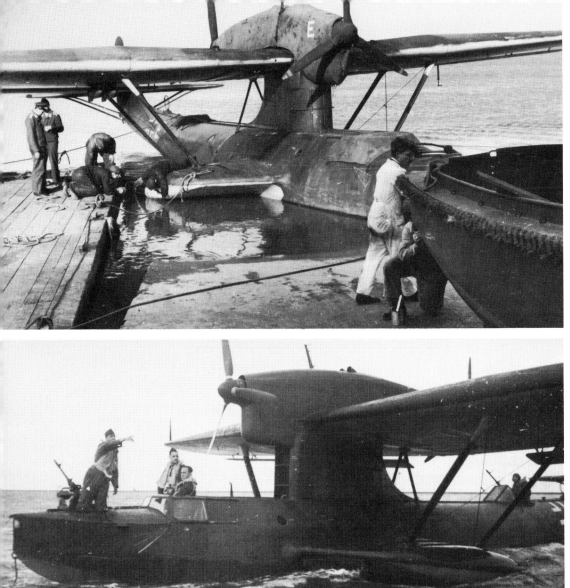

**Above left** The covers for this Do 18D's engine cowlings carry the aircraft's individual code letter. Two small bombs can be seen just outboard of the starboard wing struts (344/713/13).

**Left** Although lacking a useful maximum or cruising speed, the Do 18 was pleasant to handle both in the air and on the water. It was used a great deal for reconnaissance and air-sea rescue duties where its endurance helped to offset its other shortcomings. The bow gunner of this D–1 has obviously spotted something of importance and calls the rest of the crew's attention to it (622/2973/26).

**Below left** The gunner's attention was probably attracted by the tender which is shown arriving in this view of the same aircraft . . . (622/2973/23).

**Above** . . . and takes it in tow. It seems likely that the aircraft had suffered some form of mechanical failure as the Do 18 was quite capable of moving about this type of sea under its own steam (622/2973/33).

**Right** On arrival in harbour the aircraft is prepared to be lifted from the water and a crewman attaches the lifting shackle to the hoist point, under the watchful eye of a Hauptgefreiter who also attends the tow (622/2973/39).

**Overleaf** The engine-mounted lifting points, water rudder, wing aerial masts, bow-mounted machine-gun and cockpit hatches are some of the points worth noting on this Do 18D–1 of 3/Kü Fl Gr 406. This unit was among those later equipped with the G–1 version in which the dorsal open gun position was replaced by a turret carrying a 20 mm MG 151 cannon (MW/5611/19a).

**Above** A busy scene at a flying boat base as a Do 18D–1 of 3/Kü Fl Gr 406 has some minor work carried out to its starboard sponson. Two other mechanics busy themselves with a tender while three men, who are possibly part of the aircraft's crew, hold a discussion under the wing (344/713/12).

**Below** There seems to be some apprehension on the part of the man in the cockpit as the forward Jumo 205 engine of this Do 18D comes in for some close scrutiny (335/23/7).

**Above** A Mediterranean-based Do 24T–1, KK + UP, uses its outboard BMW Bramo engines to move towards its mooring. The dorsal turret houses a 20 mm Hispano-Suiza 404 cannon and the nose turret, which in this case is unarmed, would normally have housed a 7·9 mm MG 15 (425/306/27).

**Below** The Do 24T seen in the previous photograph has now arrived safely at its mooring. It is interesting to compare the two photographs as the light clearly affects the colour tones and in particular makes the white fuselage band and engine cowlings look entirely different in each case. The aircraft in the background is a Vichy navy Laté 298D (430/696/6a).

**Above** Slight blurring of the two outer propellers shows that these are idling although the centre engine is doing all the work in moving this Do 24T–1 (636/4054/2a).

**Below** The wake from a passing tender gently rocks this Do 24 which is securely attached to its mooring buoy. The cooling gills on the centre engine have been left in the open position (498/25/28a).

**Above** Easy access to the three BMW Bramo 323R–2 engines of the Do 24T was achieved by hinged cowlings, two per engine, which were lowered to form access steps. This picture also shows the entry hatches to the hull and the 20 mm dorsal turret (441/1363/17a).

**Below** Floatplane and flying boat share the same mooring. A Do 24 and Fokker T VIII at rest in the Aegean (439/1294/35a).

**Above** The Do 24T sat low in the water so it was essential at take-off that all hatches and windows were secure; the sit of the aircraft and the proximity to the sea of some of its hatches are plain to see in this view of a Mediterranean-based aircraft (431/721/15a).

**Below** There is a magical air of solitude as the morning mist reveals another day in the life of this Do 24 (498/25/2a).

**Above** The rear gunner's position was well exposed high between the twin-fins/rudders of the Do 24. The turret was armed with a 7·9 mm MG 15. The float and wing in the foreground belong to a Bv 138 (499/56/31).

**Below** The white Middle East tactical band has been painted out on the fuselage of this Do 24T whose dorsal turret and cannon installation is very clear. The cannon had a very low rate of fire but its rounds were telling when they hit the target (421/721/8a).

**Left** This is a Do 24V–2 pressed into service in Norway as a transport aircraft, it served with KG zbV108 SEE and was the forerunner of the more familiar radial-engined versions (MW/5620/14a).

**Below** Well protected against the elements these two crewmen await to go ashore from the stub wing of the Do 24V–2 operating in Norwegian waters (MW/5620/28a).

**Right** Spiral spinner decor was not the prerogative of the Jagd-geschwader, as is evidenced by this Do 24T–1 photographed at its Mediterranean anchorage (531/2716/31).

**Below right** A pair of float-equipped Ju 52s share a berth with a Do 24T–1. All these air-craft had a tremendous load-carrying capacity both in men and stores. During the evacuation of Crete and the Dodecan-ese Do 24s carried a load of 24 men, each of whom had 66 lb of equipment (531/2716/30a).

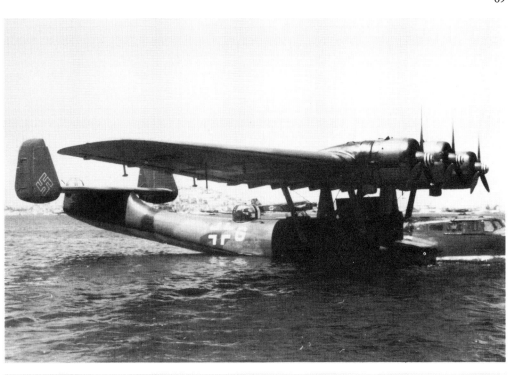

**Above** Familiar shape in perhaps slightly unfamiliar surroundings. The workhorse of the Luftwaffe transport units, the evergreen Ju 52 was modified to floatplane configuration and used in Norway, the Aegean and Mediterranean (344/713/28).

**Below** A Ju 52/3mg6e (SEE) of Seetransportstaffel 1 operating in Crete late in 1943 (526/2301/25a).

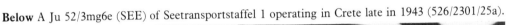

**This page** The familiar corrugated skin of the Ju 52, its peculiarly outward-pointed engines, and other endearing characteristics, are all clearly portrayed on this floatplane version whose 'sealegs' act as ideal disembarking points for the German soldiers (528/2369/10a, 22a).

**Above left** This Ju 52/3mg5e carries two-tone green upper surface camouflage, simplified national markings and a white tactical marking. Among those waiting to go aboard from the shingle beach of one of the Greek islands, are some walking wounded (528/2369/31a).

**Left** It seems that local labour has been recruited to unload supplies from this Ju 52 which is being used to bring relief to the island's garrison (529/2381/23).

**Below left** The two-tone green upper surface camouflage is very evident on this Ju 52 operating among the Greek islands. The white figures on the fin are the aircraft's work number which, in this case, is 7234, the small markings below the narrow window forward of the fuselage cross are 66 (528/2368/25).

**Above** Low down over the sea this Ju 52 photographed from a similar machine scurries towards Crete. The dorsal-mounted 7·9 mm machine-gun offered only token defence if the aircraft happened to be caught by fighters (529/2394/36a).

**Below and overleaf top** Port and starboard views of a Ju 52/3mg6e(MS). The large ring was an electrified metal alloy structure assembled in parts on the aircraft and supported by bracings under the wings and fuselage. A voltage was passed through the ring which created an electromagnetic field which exploded any magnetic mines (643/4755/30a and 37a).

**Below left** Close-up of part of the metal ring carried by the minesweeping Ju 52s. This photograph also serves to show the splinter camouflage in two tones of green carried on the top surfaces of this particular aircraft (643/4755/28a).

**Below** Minesweeping Ju 52/3mg6e(MS) en route to the search area (643/4755/7a).

**Right** Blohm and Voss built some enormous flying boats for the Luftwaffe, the best known probably being the Wiking. This Bv 222V–7 was the fourth A-O airframe fitted with Jumo diesel engines intended for the C-series boats. This particular aircraft which is camouflaged in 72/73/65, is coded X4 + CH and entered service with Aufklärungsstaffel (SEE) 222 in August 1943 (667/7142/2a).

**Right** The Bv 227V–7 spanned 150 feet 11 inches and had a length of 119 feet 9 inches. The wing turrets which carried a 20 mm cannon apiece, can be seen between the outboard and inner engines (667/7141/4a).

**Below** The neatly faired engines and smooth skinning of the Bv 222V–7 are a credit to its designers and would not have been out of place on many a post-war aircraft. The dorsal turret houses a 20 mm MG 151 cannon (667/7141/7a).

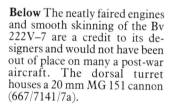

**Above** At the time of its maiden flight the Bv 238V–1 was the heaviest aircraft to have flown in the world. It is seen here on Lake Schaal in April 1944 and it was at this mooring where it was destroyed by strafing P51s of the USAAF (667/7142/24a).

**Below** The Bv 222 Wiking, was used to ferry troops from Sicily to Tunisia by the Luftransportstaffel (SEE) 222 whose Viking ship badge can be seen below the cockpit of this aircraft which is using its outboard engines to move to the jetty (6213/3002/37a).

**Above** The Blohm and Voss badge can be seen on the nose of this Bv 222 of LTS 222. As a result of combat experience later versions of the flying boat had their defensive armament increased and excluded the fixed forward firing 7·9 mm machine-gun seen above the nose hatch (623/3003/5a).

**Below** The smooth contours of the nose of the Bv 222V3 showing the initial armament arrangement of the first A series aircraft. Removal of the fixed machine-gun resulted in a much smoother line as can be seen in the next photograph (6213/3002/7a).

**Above** X4 + DH the first pre-production A-series Wiking at anchor in the Mediterranean (433/864/7).

**Below and above right** The closely cowled BMW Bramo Fafnir 323R nine-cylinder engines of the Bv 222V 4 A-series flying boat, and the unusual wing tip float design, underline the advanced state of flying boat and aircraft design in general in Germany during World War 2. In many cases designers were not allowed to proceed at the pace they would have liked, with the result that new ideas and innovations often had to give way to priority production which in some cases involved obsolete designs (433/864/5 and 12a).

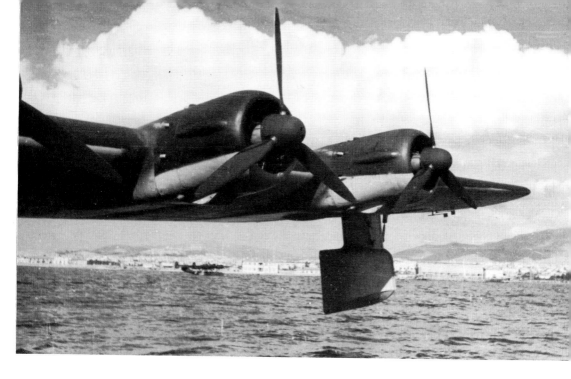

**Below and next page** This series of photographs graphically illustrates the cavernous interior of the Bv 222, in this case X4 + DH, during its service with LTS (SEE) 222. The flight deck, navigator's chart table, and wireless operator's station, show a neat and uncluttered approach which was not too usual in World War 2 aircraft. The upholstered seats add an air of luxury which must surely have been greatly appreciated by those crews lucky enough to operate this large and modern-looking flying boat (433/863/3a, 28, 24 and 21).

**Above** Arado Ar 196A–3 of 5 Bd Fl St/196 (528/2368/26).

**Below** Operating from island bases in the Aegean 2/SAGr 125 flew their Ar 196A–3s over many thousands of miles of ocean providing escort, reconnaissance and search-and-rescue facilities. The full code of this particular aircraft is 7R + HK (440/1310/12a).

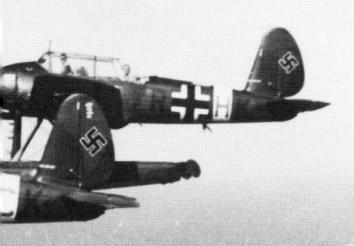

**Background photograph** A pair of Ar 196A–3s of 2/SAGr 125 on patrol. The white markings above the swastika on 7R + CK record successful attacks against coastal shipping (441/1362/31).

**Inset above left** Ar 196A–3 7R + CK of 2/SAGr 125 stands silent sentinel as its two-man crew are briefed by another officer who is possibly the Stafelkåpitan. The aircraft has 'kill' markings above its rudder swastika and is, in fact, the same machine shown in a previous air-to-air view (440/1310/29a).

**Inset above** The two officers to the right, wearing service dress hats, are both Majors, next to them is a Leutnant who is possibly the aide of the Oberstleutnant (Wing Commander) walking next to him. The aircraft is an Ar 196A–3 coded D1 + LN and is serving with SAGr 126 (530/2531/9).

**Above** The long greenhouse style canopy together with its sliding rails and hand grips, provide useful details for modellers who might be contemplating a large-scale model of the Ar 196. The hoop indicates a 'kick-in' step and the small red cross is the storage for first-aid equipment (528/2368/33).

**Below** Oil for the BMW 132K nine-cylinder air-cooled engine of this Ar 196 is poured from what seems to be a rather precarious position. The aircraft is carrying a 110 lb SC 50 bomb on its port wing rack. Each float could carry 66 gallons of fuel, which is being pumped up in this picture. They could also be used to carry spare ammunition and food containers (440/1310/30a).

**Above** The background conveys most people's thoughts about Norway; sun on snow always makes a nice photograph but it was no doubt viewed in a different light by those who had the task of moving this Ar 196 down the slipway (514/363/15a).

**Below** The aesthetically pleasing lines of Arado's Ar 196 are conveyed by this aircraft which rests on its land trolley. The huge floats were divided into seven watertight compartments and served as fuel tanks (527/2340/32a).

**Left** Two crewmen show little concern for the direction in which their Do 24T is being towed, presumably content to leave this early part of the operational sortie to the tender's crew. The aircraft is being moved out of harbour to a clear stretch of water for its take-off run (425/306/6).

**Above** Gently does it, seem to be the watchwords for this crew guiding an Ar 196 of SAGr 128 down a slipway at Brest in 1943 (609/1919/5a).

**Below** The angled radio mast attached to the frame of the pilot's windscreen was a characteristic of the Ar 196 which is very evident in this shot of an aircraft being moored in somewhat choppy conditions (530/2531/19).

**Above** An Ar 196A–3 of 4/Bordfliegergruppe 196 (T3 + NH) aboard the *Scharnhorst* (MW/5570/8).

**Below** The sea-horse badge of Bordfliegergruppe 196 can be seen on the cowling of this Ar 196A–3 which is being hoisted aboard the *Scharnhorst* (MW/5515/9a).

**Above** The observer's view of his pilot in an Ar 196 which seems to be flying a patrol as escort to a Bv 138 (637/4197/29a).

**Below** The flying crew prepare to take their stations as this Ar 196A–3 of SAGr 125 is eased into the water. The machine-gun in the rear cockpit is a 7·9 mm MG 15. The aircraft also carried two 20 mm MG FF cannon with 60 rpg and another 7·9 mm MG 15 fixed to fire forward (527/21340/37a).

**Above** The coal scuttle helmet of the man on the extreme left seems a little out of place when compared with the other headgear. But then he is standing nearest the propeller! (527/2341/7a).

**Below** Bordfliegerstaffel 1/196 was originally at Wilhelmshaven then moved to Stavanger as part of Luftflotte 5. One of its Ar 196s is shown here well battened down against the elements (624/3094/20).

**Right and overleaf top** This He 60c (IB + AH) was photographed in Finland. It has yellow wing tips and was serving with Luftflotte 5. The man sweeping snow from the wings has unconventional but efficient dress, and the item to the right of his broom is the aircraft's wind-driven generator (353/1601/8 and 9).

**Below** Showing its relationship to the Ju 52 this Junkers W 34 was being used as a communications aircraft in Norway when it caught the cameraman's eye (506/93/6).

# 1. Aircraft used in maritime operations

**Arado Ar 196 A-3**

| | |
|---|---|
| Span: | 40 feet 8 inches. Length: 36 feet 1 inch. |
| Engine: | One BMW 132K nine-cylinder, air-cooled radial. |
| Armament: | Two 20 mm MG FF cannon and one 7·9 mm MG 17 firing forward, plus one 7·9 mm MG 15 on a flexible mounting. |
| Max speed: | 194 mph. |
| Service ceiling: | 22,960 feet. |

**Blohm and Voss Ha 138**

| | |
|---|---|
| Span: | 88 feet 7 inches. Length: 65 feet $3\frac{1}{2}$ inches. |
| Engines: | Three Junkers 205D six-cylinder, liquid-cooled engines. |
| Armament: | One 20 mm MG 151 cannon in bow turret, one similar cannon in tail turret, one 13 mm MG 131 machine-gun in the dorsal turret aft of the centre engine, and one 7·9 mm MG 15 in the hull. |
| Max speed: | 177 mph. |
| Service ceiling | 31,967 feet. |
| Range: | 2,670 miles. |

**He 115**

| | |
|---|---|
| Span: | 72 feet 2 inches. Length: 56 feet 9 inches. |
| Engines: | Two BMW 132K nine-cylinder, air-cooled radials. |
| Armament: | Three 7·9 mm MG 17 machine-guns, and one 15 mm MG 151 cannon. |
| Max speed: | 180 mph. |
| Service ceiling: | 16,950 feet. |
| Range: | 1,550 miles. |

---

# 2. Some German maritime units and their aircraft

| | |
|---|---|
| 1 /Kü Fl Gr 106 | He 59, He 60, He 115 |
| 2 /Kü Fl Gr 106 | Do 18 |
| 3 /Kü Fl Gr 106 | He 59, He 115 |
| 1 /Kü Fl Gr 406 | He 60, He 59, Do 18, He 115, Bv 138 |
| 1 /Kü Fl Gr 506 | He 114, He 115 |
| 2 /Kü Fl Gr 506 | Ar 196, He 114 |
| 3 /Kü Fl Gr 506 | He 115 |
| 1 /Kü Fl Gr 706 | Ar 196, Do 59, He 115, Bv 138 |

| | |
|---|---|
| 1&2 /Kü Fl Gr 906 | He 114, He 115, Do 18, Bv 138 |
| 3 /Kü Fl Gr 906 | He 114 |
| 1,2,3 /KG 200 | He 59, He 60, He 115, Ar 196 |
| SAGr 125 | Ar 95, Ar 196, He 114 |
| SAGr 126 | Ar 95, Ar 196, He 114 |
| SAGr 127 | Ar 95 |
| SAGr 128 | Ar 196 |
| SAGr 130 | Ar 196, Bv 222, Bv 138 |
| III /KG 100 | Ar 196 |
| KG 26 | He 111H-6 |
| KG 30 | He 111H-6 |
| KG 40 | FW 200 |

The above are only typical units and aircraft operated by them on occasions during World War 2. It is not intended to be definitive or to include all units and all aircraft used in maritime roles.

# ACHTUNG! COMPLETED YOUR COLLECTION?

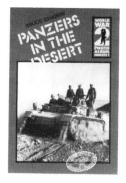

## Other titles in the same series

**No 1 Panzers in the Desert**
*by Bruce Quarrie*

**No 2 German Bombers over England**
*by Bryan Philpott*

**No 3 Waffen-SS in Russia**
*by Bruce Quarrie*

**No 4 Fighters Defending the Reich**
*by Bryan Philpott*

**No 5 Panzers in North-West Europe**
*by Bruce Quarrie*

**No 6 German Fighters over the Med**
*by Bryan Philpott*

**No 7 German Paratroops in the Med**
*by Bruce Quarrie*

**No 8 German Bombers over Russia**
*by Bryan Philpott*

**No 9 Panzers in Russia 1941–43**
*by Bruce Quarrie*

**No 10 German Fighters over England**
*by Bryan Philpott*

**No 11 U-Boats in the Atlantic**
*by Paul Beaver*

**No 12 Panzers in Russia 1943–45**
*by Bruce Quarrie*

**No 13 German Bombers over the Med**
*by Bryan Philpott*

**No 14 German Capital Ships**
*by Paul Beaver*

**No 15 German Mountain Troops**
*by Bruce Quarrie*

**No 16 German Fighters over Russia**
*by Bryan Philpott*

**No 17 E-Boats and Coastal Craft**
*by Paul Beaver*

## In preparation

**No 19 Panzers in the Balkans and Italy**
*by Bruce Quarrie*

**No 20 German Destroyers and Escorts**
*by Paul Beaver*

# ACHTUNG! COMPLETED YOUR COLLECTION?